Rubaiyat from a Floating Life

by

Don Moore, Jr.

"Rubaiyat from a Floating Life," by Don Moore Jr. ISBN 978-1-951985-16-5 (softcover); 978-1-951985-17-2 (hardcover); 978-1-951985-18-9 (eBook).

Library of Congress Number on file with publisher.

Published 2020 by Virtualbookworm.com Publishing Inc., P.O. Box 9949, College Station, TX 77845, US. ©2020 Don Moore Jr. All rights reserved. No part of this publication may be reproduced, stored in a retrieval system, or transmitted in any form or by any means, electronic, mechanical, recording or otherwise, without the prior written permission of Don Moore Jr.

Don Moore, Jr.

October 11, 1944 – February 26, 2019

Don Moore had the soul of a poet. Inspired by mathematician, astronomer, poet Omar Khayyam, he penned ***Rubaiyat from a Floating Life***. Written in 1974, his 101 quatrain poem is appropriate in today's world. Using a Persian rhyme scheme to write his four line stanzas, Don espoused some of the same concepts depicted in Khayyam's rubaiyat: the love of nature and coping with life.

Don was the author of one published book of poetry, ***The Ballad of Ned Kelly and Lyrics from the Rustic Lyre***. He also contributed to various newsletters over the years, the most recent being the ***Lexicom***, a publication of Bluegrass Mensa in Lexington, Kentucky. As a stocks and commodity trader, he used his knowledge of mathematics, ephemeris, and historic economic cycles in his business, perhaps as Khayyam might have. Although a constant student of the universe, his talent belonged in the world of words: lyrics, poems, sonnets, witticisms, and limericks. He and Omar Khayyam would have been great friends.

I

Look up! The wind has caught this kite of mine
Propelling it on Khayyam's lilting line
To where it hangs suspended, falls, and floats
Off toward horizons lit in hues of wine.

II

When loud of This and That the people shout,
I ask once more, "What is it all about?"
And to the Garden tranquil-made retire;
How else confront how many years of doubt?

III

And there a rapt simplicity takes shape;
How now of him or her to idly ape?
For yet within the Garden tarry these;
O let me go with Khayyam–and his Grape.

IV

A special talent throned within the heart,

A special vision where the eyebrows part,

But grant me these, my Lovely, if you will,

And O, my vagabonding will be short!

V

At once the happy thought doth herald flight,

And the sage traveler always travels light,

Sloughs off the bag and baggage of the past

And piece by piece the armor 'gainst old fright.

VI

Free from the tyrannies of useless form,

Relax; ask not "What is Today's fresh norm?"

The endless flux will bring it round again

And let it some Tomorrow too deform.

VII

And so, my friends, I hoped I had one want.

But one. The rest? Why, let them elsewhere taunt.

For where I go how can they follow me

Through the far Country of the Nonchalant?

VIII

Come where the falling cataracts the Voice

Of Many waters echo, there to deep rejoice,

Ensconced at ease upon a mossy rock

Where the misty mountain with the sky alloys.

IX

What is the news of Summer? Some the Spring

Let pass and did not hear the small birds sing;

And other news may Autumn supersede–

To leave but Winter's last cold reckoning.

X

Now Nature's monk not <u>from</u>, but <u>to</u>, does flee
And bathes his five fine senses: Debauchee,
That robe of sequined green she wears for you!
Come to her breast and taste–serenity.

XI

Long ages past, the glaciers came and hurled
Huge mountains up above where wild waves curled
Their foamy fingers round the settling shore–
And for the nonce it's "Welcome to the World."

XII

Creation's left hand, O, but can impress!
But with her right hand, Ah! That fond caress
Envelopes every bank of flowerets,
The smallest bud to reassure and bless.

XIII

The clouds, with shadows, entertain the trees;
The wistful willow bends before the breeze;
Cicadas drowsily with chirps intone
Their homely song, and put me at my ease.

XIV

Into the glade, a quietude achieving,
I go a day, but then a moment's grieving
And all is flown. Then wafts it back again,
A moment's peace some other day retrieving.

XV

If nothing matters of the HERE nor THERE,
Why did Thoreau to Walden Pond repair?
Or Whitman, that old seeker of the Self,
Lie in those leaves of grass full many a day?

XVI

Old Eagles elsewhere feed upon the heart,

While common Harpies tear the mind apart,

To lean and loaf, a Fellow of the Clouds'

And Waters' Byways, is, for me,-a start.

XVII

The dreary haunts of men who mind the store:

Square straight shapes of buildings, they make poor

Stuff for the Spirit's gaming Guide who may

Shake clean his dusty feet and quit your door.

XVIII

Adventure where the petals deepest strewn

Are seen by light, though feeble, of the moon.

That paly moon will set, as bright the day

Breaks o'er our East of Eden–late or soon!

XIX

I ever did despair to know the bliss

That tumbles down the earth-built edifice,

Entertaining the One–I know not Whom–

With the mockery of our Genesis.

XX

I seek the WHAT, not knowing WHO is tasking,

And ask, while in such ignorance yet basking,

The WHY, until a voice within replies:

"O the absurd vanity of asking!"

XXI

It pains to hear again the timeworn story,

How weak-willed EVE had ADAM taste the glory

The serpent offered up from out a tree,

A tree of some old poet's allegory.

XXII

For still that subtle beast in back of me
Goads on my EVE, my ADAM, and the three
Have left my system's tree a tangled web,
And me–to till the dust through history.

XXIII

Words are like blowing leaves and scriptures cramp
The few and true discernments that the Scamp
Along the way proves on his pulse. O fie
On verse that smells unduly of the lamp!

XXIV

But come and gaze where Beauty yet does grace
The All-in-all, with Truth to interlace,
Where dreaming Poe toward his far wandering star
Reaches out–and Keats turns his wasting face.

XXV

Our memories are but a flickering gleam

From a deep light: Things are not all they seem,

And yet, and yet a moment here, create,

Try, stumble, Ha! Now sink to sleep-and dream.

XXVI

They say the realms of dreamers duplicate

That Heav'n where Angels at a touch create;

But there these spread white wings of gossamer,

Themselves to seek a <u>dreamless</u> sleep–their fate.

XXVII

Another verse? Leave till tomorrow morn.

And music? Tones die on the string stillborn.

And riddles? They, too, of this world, may see

Me leave it as I entered it–forlorn.

XXVIII

How many days know not our glad adieus?

So think, what do the Poor in Spirit lose

To bid farewell to future days betimes

And with discrimination at last choose?

XXIX

Come! Where the bright light of dawn is breaking.

Drink! Where Khayyam oft his thirst was slaking.

Or will a thousand thousand years of dawns

Pass, each yielded to–an undertaking?

XXX

And if, my friend, the burden that you bear

Allow one moment for a question, <u>where</u>

Carry you on your heavy load of <u>what</u>–

They shout, "O, it's impractical to care."

XXXI

But this I know: There are events that prick
The stubborn Ego through its costumes thick
To almost evanesce and leave but what
Knows pleasure still as carrot, pain as stick.

XXXII

This oscillating Globe will see repeat
Those twin imposters, Vict'ry and Defeat,
Until one lesson, followed by one more,
Build up to where man cries like Lear–"Retreat."

XXXIII

Let one with tears carve out his epitaph
And yet another sob on his behalf.
For me this same and little drama brings
Pain, pleasure, yes, but after all–a laugh.

XXXIV

The laugh is mine when Ripeness like a shawl
Descends; one thing I know, <u>my</u> pleasures pall;
One thing I know, that Prompter, Pain, may call
And leave his venomed card–a draught of gall.

XXXV

But if what we call HOME is but a cell,
And we adrift from our true Home, then–well,
We here, uneasy visitors, must ask:
"What in it shall we touch and take–pray tell?"

XXXVI

Ah, there's the query with which man won't part,
Dear to the pontiff's and pundit's heart.
But not to any but myself I turn
To hear: "Nothing. For nothing's what thou art."

XXXVII

The actor acts, but all the props he buys
Can never alter his last scene–he dies,
His role is written out, his lines forgot,
His gear is gone, and worms feed on his eyes.

XXXVIII

Who plays for plaudits of an audience
That proffers praise and blame to make him wince,
Think, aren't these extras in the selfsame cast?
They throng the boxes as impertinence!

XXXIX

Beyond the footlights in the dark is missed
The subtle promptings of that Dramatist
Who seems to hold in hand some other script–
Play to him Him: In the end He will insist.

XL

What! Actors all not knowing what was writ

In the true play, and all its opposite

Inbred at birth, applauded from the pit,

And sold as drama of the infinite?

XLI

Whether from out the void and cursed with crime

Or born to fill a form evolved from slime,

I stumble with the curtain up once more

And for a redirection ask but–Time.

XLII

The Time that knows the rose as child of Spring,

And bright daisy's Summer coloring,

Beyond whose charm the Fall chrysanthemum

With a laugh sets the season partying.

XLIII

When Time awhile his willful steeds unyokes,
When the tea is brewed and the incense smokes,
We sit and talk of art.–Alas, that poems
And paintings go no deeper than their looks.

XLIV

The cloud takes color from the daylight rays;
Toward cliffs the rivulet meandering strays
To so become a waterfall: Thus act
On me my friends of free and easy ways.

XLV

To stroll along the river arm in arm
And let some weeping willow there disarm
Us of each sore contrivance in the heart,
Where a breeze blowing lengthens out the charm.

XLVI

And the long afternoon through which we go

Leads simply to a shaded portico,

And there, enchanted, we forget ourselves,

As the Spring meadow-grass forgets the snow.

XLVII

With such old friends, to try the season's teas

Is to watch as the third boil gently frees

Juice of dawn-picked leaves: such fine distinctions!

Would that there were some finer still than these.

XLVIII

The tower-topped castle by the lake lives twice;

Ah, Sweet, <u>one</u> only better would suffice.

And every dry mirage the desert wears

Can only hint of water–and entice.

XLIX

The happy black bee has the lotus sweet,

And we? <u>This</u> universe is at our feet.

Could but a poet from a pot of verse

Divine a purpose in such gross deceit!

L

The thoughtful fellow queries, "What to do?"

Well, there must be worse thoughts to think and rue.

The camel that with bloody mouth chews thorns:

Indeed, I know not what to do with you!

LI

To start some Path marked RIGHT and WRONG,

Implies a distance although, all along,

Within, that Bird of Golden Plumage sits

And in low volume sings an unheard song.

LII

Of all the Good and Bad we doff and don

With hope of the nine planets lost or won,

Of all the flux of basic pain, forget!

Our sins are of the past–and it is gone.

LIII

Host old philosophers–yes, like as not–

When it comes down to it, their system's shot.

The fight you fight is yours to fight alone,

Fight! And you'll not recall you ever fought.

LIV

Alas, to chain the Fancy's daft pretense

And leave it quite without an audience;

But trade it quick, friend, for experience!

The transcendental conch shell blows. Commence!

LV

The lines of least resistance bristle, fraught

With face cards of compulsion, overwrought

With deuces of desire that dance and march

To task me with their trumpet call "Take thought."

LVI

But when the pasteboard jack or king that blew

The trumpet, from within the fifty-two

Spoke up, "To shuffle us is natural,"

At that, I stuck the deck back in the shoe.

LVII

Tis all a card trick where the player vies

From a wild and scattered deck to pluck the prize,

And as the heedless pips dance on the green

Felt board – the Joker laughs, the player cries.

LVIII

And from the outset did I comprehend

That on my skill alone all would depend.

But, brother, shut the door: This trick is hard

Enough without the worry of the wind!

LIX

Now the next morn revives the same old yearnings,

And part and parcel seem they of Earth's turnings,

For round and round, binary night and day

Whip up a whirlpool of unending churnings.

LX

What, sweetly tasting, turns to poison soon,

And, in the bloodstream, ends in deathly swoon?

What, hard to swallow, melts to mellow mead,

And, in the heart, bestows the sweetest boon?

LXI

Ah, Khayyam, oft across your verse enshrined
My eyes have gone where your whole being wined,
And till my every atom drinks, my mind
Alone must quaff <u>this</u> draught: no axe to grind.

LXII

A Dervish proffered drugs for what I lacked:
"They do expand the mind and that's a fact."
But what have little I to do with mind
More than with my big toe? O, mind, contract!

LXIII

What next will that gray prodigy dispute?
Listen to this. One day stretched at the foot
Of an aged apple tree, I saw it
Bowing to me, bent low with ripened fruit;

LXIV

And bowing back, what part of me could grudge,
I wondered; then I gave the tree a nudge
And murmured, "Lucky, naught in thee there is
That either thee or me would deign to judge."

LXV

A fire perhaps there is to cauterize
What deep subconscious habit grooves arise
Within, but ever where there's fire there's smoke-
And further blackened is that realm of lies.

LXVI

Again one day within the glade I saw
A tortoise who regarded me with awe,
And as I stealthily upon him crept,
I watched his head and his four legs withdraw.

LXVII

Another in that wood, a recluse flown,
I glimpsed who into <u>his</u> own shell had gone
It seemed; but yet a different animal
He soon appeared—when I tossed out a bone!

LXVIII

I think the Goths who Rome thrice sacked
Are not so far removed from us; in fact,
The selfsame stuff that drove them on is just
The glue that holds <u>my</u> makeshift form intact.

LXIX

But he who shakes his head and backward peers
As well could at the future aim his jeers,
And vow to never see the same again
Across the four and twenty thousand years.

LXX

Bright candles of desire the daylight flout,

But see, the longest burning are about

Burnt to the nub. To those of newer cast

Reach up, and with seared fingers snuff them out.

LXXI

Ah, my Beloved, play me like a flute,

While all these myriad duties that recruit

And have recruited me before to act

Let go of me–as I let go their fruit.

LXXII

Indeed, indeed, all action to forswear

Did I once wish and of it did despair

Till in the dust my briny tears spelt out

Somber words: "Not while you breathe Earth's air."

LXXIII

Then if I may, another anecdote:
First weren't it better that the vessel float
Seaworthy on its way than water rush
Through ratholes and so inundate the boat?

LXXIV

O let me on the river hoist the sail
Where would the swimmer, wildly gasping, flail
His helpless arms, once more to, weighted down,
Drown in that riptide's tormenting travail.

LXXV

To the four winds and to unerring Fate
I'll turn the strife-torn craft and then, My Mate,
Whither we go I will not ask, nor act
In aught but what to Thee I dedicate.

LXXVI

Hither and yon the infant kitten goes.

By the scruff of its neck the mother stows

The little creature safe between her teeth.

What utter relaxation that it knows!

LXXVII

For sure that one does not a CREED profess.

Picture it, poet: one obsession less,

From out the wrangle yet I hear it, yes:

"Quasi modo geniti infantes."

LXXVIII

The Prophets who have trod our dusty lands

And left behind a blessing, their commands

Ring true for us as them. But Lo! They cast

No shadow and walk trackless through the sands.

LXXIX

And still our journey started long ago,
And still as then, etched on some vast tableau,
Our end is theirs, and our beginning too,
Like the sacred rivers' interminable flow.

LXXX

And should such Revelation move to prayers
About some realm of nine and forty layers
The passerby beside the bough and book,
I ask with cup in hand, "Who knows–or cares?"

LXXXI

If the whole bundle of what men have penned
As Truth were offered, I'd instead say, "Send
Not what the mind can comprehend, but that
<u>By which</u>, dear friend, the mind doth comprehend."

LXXXII

Think, all the ones who come to Earth's way station
Know but the rise and fall of tribulation,
Lacking the ALL they will be, knowing not
They NOW are, turning to–imagination.

LXXXIII

And if that cinema, that film you view
Turns to insipid trash as all films do,
Bringing the three dimensions down to two,
Then simply switch it off, and you be YOU.

LXXXIV

Out from the world an image in your eyes,
Distorted where the mind may tyrannize,
Turns MARE to MARES-NEST under your nose;
Say you above, "I'm watching."–Ah, it flies.

LXXXV

And when as automatically as ON,
The OFF has rendered you a fool, anon
That MARE who all the time was munching grass
Neighs; and–that old illusion-screen is gone.

LXXXVI

Yes, what significance was ever in
REACTION dogging ACTION as a twin?
But now with pure attention crystallized,
Hie homeward deeper, devotee, within.

LXXXVII

The Whole, they say, is held within the Part,
And both, behind Time, timeless as pure Art;
But please, no further of this talk, my friend–
And thereby leave the horse behind the cart!

LXXXVIII

Away! To relativity assign

The tumbling dots and dies that would combine

To number out the point of a Divine

You cannot hit. High-rollers! Call for wine.

LXXXIX

The Wine that like a lodestar weans one from

The taunt of this and that palladium,

Ambrosial nectar which who finds is found,

Like a lost line of some unfinished poem.

XC

As much as Words have been my coterie

Thoughts composed of them have played with me,

My Vintner is the only friend I have

Who neither wants–nor gives–idolatry.

XCI

You know, the Consciousness I would embrace
May all my status in the world efface.
To thread a needle: solitary lot!
And what, then, if one fiber's out of place?

XCII

Perk up. A child into the morn awakes
And robed in his own Wonder's kingly flakes
Asks Nature, "What–what *is* it that you hold?"
And not till night the mystery forsakes.

XCIII

O Thou who Man to dwarfed mentality
Scattered–as a star scatters hot debris,
Thou, wilt, assure, alike a quasar, draw
Him back, as draws the cresting wave the sea;

XCIV

As draws the momentary wave the sea

To the mirror-glass of eternity;

And if the wave that tries to measure Thee

Melt before the measure, well–let it be.

XCV

O Man who yesterday, to overturn

Your instincts and a scrap of knowledge earn

Today, decided what to grasp or spurn–

You left your Intuition this: to yearn!

XCVI

O Thou who made the lightning and the thunder

And rendered indescribable the wonder

Storms, clouds, all make; wouldst Thou conceive

It whole–to see it piecemeal torn asunder?

XCVII

Clouds through blueness, blues in cloudness sail.

Beside the barn door rusts the same old nail.

Sans such exotic ballet it would be

A long long afternoon behind the veil.

XCVIII

Ah, friends, could we imbibe beneath the trees,

Kissing goodbye a string a memories,

Together–knowers, known all one–to taste

Of what the elder poet writes –and sees!

XCIX

Some in the Net have shrunk themselves so small

To one day noiselessly to Freedom fall,

And some expanded till it could not hold

And burst.–Ah, Faith, is such the end of all?

C

So Darling, if you see some snare entrap

Me, take my anguished head upon your lap

And gently, Sister, gently in my ear

Hum soft such songs as can my Soul enwrap.

CI

Whether this Quickening, like a two-edged knife,

Sever my bonds or deepen wounds of strife,

What was it anyhow but writing out

Another stanza of a floating life.

www.ingramcontent.com/pod-product-compliance
Lightning Source LLC
Chambersburg PA
CBHW031439040426
42444CB00006B/888